Will You Think of Me When You Dance

Marty Gammons

NEWMAN SPRINGS PUBLISHING
320 Broad Street
Red Bank, NJ 07701

First originally published by Newman Springs Publishing 2024

ISBN 979-8-89308-300-2 (Paperback)
ISBN 979-8-89308-301-9 (Digital)

Printed in the United States of America

To Niki, my daughter.

Illustrator James Penn

Will You Think of Me When You Dance

Upon the floor your feet,
Shuffle and shuffle to the beat.
Rosy smiles upon your face.
The happiest heart in the place.

Will you think of me when you dance?
I'm sure there's not a heaven's chance.
I lie motionless all alone in my bed.
As visions of you put another gun to my head.

Never did I think you would leave me.
There wasn't a chance that you would be,
The horrible slut that you became.
You made our love seem so lame.

Cry not for my broken heart
For you have made me a part.
Of the dance I dance tonight
Oh, but so soft as we take flight.

A fine line we dance in the dark
Careful not on a journey to embark.
Deeper and deeper to keep the screams quiet
Into the pillow we bury for another night's riot.

Wrapping the wounds tighter than tight.
As the gentle flow tries to win the fight.
Tonight was a little too deep
As through the cloth it seeps

Maybe too great was the plight.
For tonight could be the night.
Aside the cloth I should throw
And be not afraid to go.

Will you think of me when you dance?
As past this life I prance.
For visions of you my eyes plead.
And, my God, let the wound bleed.

It's 4 A.M.

Its 4 a.m.
The windows are locked
The doors are double locked
The hinges have been checked

I've pulled the covers tight
Tighter and tighter till I can't
Breathe

Shhhhh, hush not a sound!

And now I can't see?

Hush, please!

Where is it that they might be.
The fear is choking the life from me.

I'm awake, I'm awake, in my bed
In my bed I quake. Feel it shake!

I scream to the windows.
I scream to the walls.
To one and all, I call
But silence upon their ears fall.

Can you not hear me?
Can you not hear?
From 'neath the marsh I call.
Soaked with their pain.
A permanent bloodstain.

I call, I fall.
I fall and I call
I scream and I gleam
But my eyes have lost their beam.

I CALL

I CALL

Screams

The evening's deafening silence
Surrendered by the screams
Passionately empty walls
Footprints exploring the halls

Darkness on midday's sun
As the tears rob the fun
Empty souls deeper in the well
Devil's journey to a patient hell

Tears hidden by the smiles
Unforgettable tortuous miles
Rest not under the pine tree
To the undiscovered country flee

Fleeting kisses upon the brow
Friendship secretly disavowed
Lonely night's plea
As silence comes to be

Never-Ending Dream

Out of the darkness into my room.
Tiptoe, tiptoe, you did walk.
Not a sound, eerie did you come.
Thirst for my soul you embellished.

Upon my naked neck, chills gave.
Breathe upon the hairs of my soul,
Taunting my sleep, laughter cried.
Screech, screech tiny voice whined.

Awake, awake sleep no more!
My eyes open not, fear lock closed.
Pillow drowning, at the heart's plea.
While wiggle not given, urge, urge.

Frozen ice in your shallow veins.
Tempestuous smile upon the brow.
Avalanche of growls piercing night.
Breast torn open and heart taken.

Silence

Silence, silence gasp for something.
Hand nor eye from heaven fell.
Mercy, mercy upon my knees I lay.
Demons scavenge, cause not seen.

Morrow, where is thy mercy?
Weakened soul and redundancy.
Whilst in thy bed, sleep you have.
Where is thy empathy?

Soaked sheets tightly wrapped,
Embossed tears flood the night.
Upon my cheeks questions flow.
Where is thy mercy, where, oh, where?

A single night, visit not I plea.
Upon raw knees, head hung low.
Hands grasping at heaven's skirt.
Tears departing the dry soul.

Silent Prayers

The girded loins of the child,
Blessed by the mother's womb.
Upon the floor left piled,
Forever stranded, eternity's tomb.

Tireless feet across the floor roam,
Back and forth in the night.
Through the satin braids comb,
Praying for mystical sight.

Fear lingers into the sun so bright,
As darkness succumbs to day.
The mornings doves take flight,
And the future here to stay.

Memories fade to blur,
As the child fights the crows.
Into the marsh the boats stir,
As the fogs mystery grows.

She takes the wind from the sails,
As the swamp swallows time.
And the wood receives its nails.
Hidden to blinded ears of crime

Good Night, My Love

Good night, My Love
Why did you call my name?
Did you not feel any shame?
You captured my heart
And wantonly tore me apart

You gave me all I want
Now you are an evil haunt
The sex was so Divine
You kept me in perfect line

Your name rang so sweet
Now it is my bitter defeat
I scream for you at night
Only demons come to sight

For my death tonight I pray
There is no reason to stay
A lonely dream that is best
To see the blood upon my chest

As my eyes I close
This is the path I chose
Memories I can't stand
Listen to the angels' band

It is the flesh that I hate
In your arms I no more mate
Call not my name, you whore
For the blood has begun to pour

They try so hard to save
But the minutes I shave
As the day draws nigh
Gather with a final sigh

In darkness cover my pain
For my life was not in vain
Torturous love only grows
When you realize that life froze

It is with closed eyes I smile
As my feet finish the last mile
Today I love her never again
For her heart I no longer contend

Whispering Pines

Darkness hides the widow's song.
As the pines utter a sweet melody.
Buried deep 'neath the evergreens.
Hold fast the roots of dreams.

Mama cries, a song of songs!
As the world forgets who belongs.
Baby sighs, as the memory dies.
Submerged in a quaint bath of lies.

Oh, but the mystery of dark.
Hidden as the devils embark.
Silent screams on deaf ears
As witness bears through the years.

From the darkness the soul creeps
As from the night, hope rings a peep.
Gentle, mumbling words stutter
For the truth will make you shutter.

Pleading words stab the heart.
From the bones tears depart.
Breathless gentle pleas.
Lost in ever-deepening seas.

A final word upon rubber knees
Please! Please! Please!

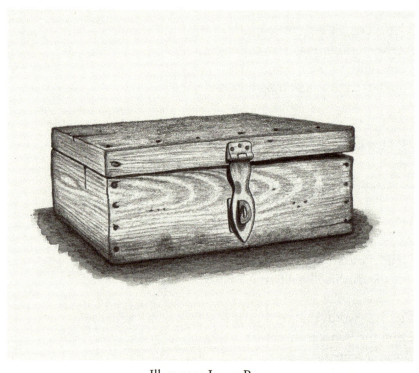

Illustrator James Penn

Not Forgotten

Tiny wooden box.
Footprint on the rocks.
Whispers to the soul,
Long forgotten goal.

Where was I, my friend?
When your life did end.
Hidden in the illusion,
Drowned in the demon's confusion.

Be patient and open thy arms.
Soon I will return to your charms.
The path is dreaded and weary,
For of this world I'm found dreary.

Oh, but the forgotten times
We were partners in crime.
The ragged heart searches
Remembering songs of churches.

The times in the hills
Buried by too many pills.
The happy dancing squeals,
To this day my heart kills.

The day soon shall be,
By my side so much glee.
Let the dirt to the side move,
And from this world remove.

Visitor

Is that you by my bed?
Or is just demons in my head?
Is it darkness that blinds?
Or is it my legs intertwined?

The shadow crossed my feet.
Another world about to meet.
The cover ripped from my soul,
As darkness brings another hole.

Wrinkled sheets curse the night,
As demons enter my sight.
Not with the eye can I see,
But deep within my head they be.

Why can't they depart,
Leaving alone my heart.
The sun soon shall rise
The pillow pressed on my thighs.

I never asked you to come,
If only you would leave a crumb.
My heart to the demons I gave
As now it becomes a slave.

Mama's Prayers

Sweet little tiny droplet,
Hypnotic hue of scarlet.
Mama's blessings and tears
Brought forth mama's fears.

Enchanting passionate journey,
Haunted by the ground wormy.
Lingering nightly prayers,
Waisted on scuffed knees' despair.

Endless rivers, midnight search,
Upon pillows, droplets perch.
Hunting for a ray of light,
Somewhere in the midst of night.

Frozen words marred by soft lips.
Screaming quietly in tiny drips.
Mama's prayer hidden in silence,
As the river forgets its guidance.

Did You Not Hear?

My screams did you not hear?
They were meant for your ear!
Night after night I called your name.
Your heart thought it a game.

The pursed demon's lips,
Wantonly followed scripts.
With each thunderous click.
The clock, my life it wicked.

My screams did you not hear?
Hands raised to heaven with a tear.
On my knees, I screamed your name.
But you slept without shame.

On my walls they knocked.
I know my doors, I locked.
In my halls they creeped.
Around each corner I peeped.

My screams did you not hear?
Why must I yell so, in fear?
Did you not hear my closed lips?
Now they come from the crypts.

The whimpers in my sleep!
But never another peep.
Did you not hear my cries?
Forever now closed my eyes.

My screams did you not hear?

Mama's Tears

Oh, sweet, sweet child,
Rest your weary heart tonight.
For the demons have compiled,
Little is left but the angels' flight.

Upon mother's bosom sleep,
And lay your sweet little head.
In her arms cry not another peep,
For the sheep have crossed the bed.

Soaking the earth, tears have fell,
Woven into tomorrow's pain,
Driven by a never-ending well,
Hidden by yesterday's stain.

Sleepless nights, smothered dreams,
Pictures in the hall upon the wall.
Ripped apart by love's seams,
As the nightmares begin to crawl.

Mama's tears in a bed of fears.
Soaked sheets and worn floors.
Mama's tears in a book of years.
Drained from the closed doors

Mirror, Mirror

Broken shards plastering time.
Nothing but pain left to rhyme.
Moments of life, left in death
Searching for the final breath

Reflections depleted to a stain
As love is left emulating pain.
One more kiss upon the brow
As the tainted lips disavow.

Morning's dew and birds' call
As the feet take to the long hall.
Brightest of lights, message sent
For the fool's broken knees, bent.

Bitterness of sweetest taste.
Such an inglorious waste.
Kneel before, as they sing
Await the golden tones ring.

Sweet Princess

From the depths of my heart,
Your trail of tears depart.
Scurrying to the grips of gravity
Devoured beneath the corpse of morality.

Your flowing crimson grips
Steal from the soul, tiny sips
Bequeath the torment of reality
Buried in the pages of legality

Where is thy mercy, my queen
As darkness sets another routine
I bow before thy journey,
As the bowels embellish wormy

If and only may I,
Plead with you as you die
Bring me home to peace,
As the rivers begin to cease

Baby's Screams

Baby's screams and silent tears.
Rooms filled with empty fears.
Deathly silence flooding the night.
Soul of blackness obscuring sight.

The golden curse killing dreams.
As the world splits at the seams.
Falling deep into nothingness.
Little left, but the devil's witness.

Baby's screams left unheard.
As the passion of love is deterred.
Baby's screams
And the glow of the beam.

Find your flowing bed.
Sturdied by the mysterious dead.
Child, Stay your course.
And ride the winged horse

Sweet, Sweet Lies

What fools' Lie is this?
Perched upon the devil's kiss
Passionately hidden so deep
Upon the wicked lips did creep

Mockery of the gilded heart
As the limbs are ripped apart
Breath by breath in time
Death shall become the crime

Oh, sultry passion-filled lips
From the blackened winds, tiny sip
As life left the tattered sleeve
The lies only proved to deceive

Let the wind scatter it to and fro
For love's sails have been stowed
No story to be told
Never again shall he be bold

What Would It Be?

What would it be?
If the rivers failed to flow to the sea.
What would it be?
If my reflection dared to look back at me.

What would it be?
To gaze through the glass door.
What would it be?
To see the blood upon the floor.

Oh, but the words.
The wicked, wicked screaming words
Oh, but the words.
Departing on the back of wingless birds.

Oh, but the words.
Marring the walls of the blackened soul.
Oh, but the words.
Pressing the light from the darkened hole.

Devour the day.
For my feet shall not come play.
Sweetly devour the day.
For after morrow night shall come to stay

Devil's Play

Perilous dictation
Hammering the strings of consequence

Devil's lullaby
Singing a song to never be sung again

Deafened ears
Screaming for a peaceful rhythm

Beg, beg no more
For tomorrow shall never see today
Keep the applause to a dull roar
For an ovation shall not honor the pleas.

As the lights dim
And the curtains close
Gather your gaze to yesterday
For tomorrow's answer can't be found today

Tomorrow

Upon the satin clouds
Rivers of black parch the night.
Rainbows fade into shadows
And the moon becomes caustic

Thirteen moons break the back
As the ground wanders about.
Tiny lakes tell a tale
And the ears hear not

What shall the owl cry?
As the crevices fill with salt
What shall the ravens devour?
As the grass grows green

How shall the pages be turned?
No story for the words to tell.
Will the tree remember the broken branch?
As the leaves fail to grow.

Will the dirt whisper to the stones?
Or shall they scream at the worms?
What shall my name become?
As tomorrow curses today

I Cried Last Night

The most perfect of dreams ensued, a perfect day of passion. The heart mangled in a fantasy that controls the very thoughts of a man. Absolute perfection was brought into his life from an unlikely source and an unlikely time. Not able to pursue the mindless thoughts of his heart, he allows sleep to overcome the day. The visions of the one that he loves makes sleep come so easy. Dreams of love passionately fill the night with near endless happiness. Wait, no longer able to sleep, the screaming silence and the beat beating of heart fill the room with an unbearable and deafening sound. Awakening, desiring to hold the one that he loves, turning, to find his arms empty once again. Tears streaming, pouring, from the battered eyes, overflowing from the broken heart, soaking the sheets, smothering the soul from his body. Quivering flesh, batting, wiping the stream from his cheeks, he sighs softly. The disgust from the world and consequences around him swallow any hope of rest. I cried last night. No one to comfort, no one to understand, no one to hold, he prays for the morning's light. Will his dreams and desires ever evolve? With the light piercing through the crack in the veil and mocking his soul, he is reminded that yet another night has passed without the one that holds a grip upon his soul.

Illustrator Bryon Redfield

Roses

Withered roses lying on the floor. A tattered stream passionately flowing from the cheek of a brokenhearted man. Years of neglect taking a heavy toll on the love once felt within the soul. Forgotten promises, memorable lies cloud the desires and dreams once felt. The preacher's words but a painful echo ringing unfaithfully in his ears. Many years of nightly desires melting into a puddle of aggression. No one remembers how or where it was lost, only that it is no longer worth it.

Creepy

Sweetest of reds
Taunting the child
Such creepy innocence
Stealing the light

Pirouetting down the promenade
Beckoning evil, silently screaming.
Torturing the curiosity
Offering imminent death.

Hilarious paint
Over the creepy soul
Gnarling teeth and an evil heart
Scouring the refuse for the lost

Conquering the night
Infallible fear of the day
Don't be afraid to come and play
For evil is here to stay

Salacious

Oh, luscious demons
Plastering salacious desires
Enticing the soul
Binding the darkest hour

Twisted sheets
Tangled around my soul
Mocking heaven's journey
With demon's delight.

Fingertips Salaciously tickling
Tender heartstrings
Pleading for a moment's light
Gasping for another breath

Passion embedded
Tiniest of thoughts
Pondering not morning's light
As the night fades to perfection.

I Love You

Pretentious words.
Mocking the soul.
Scattering the heart.
Knocking at hell's gate.

Sweetest words upon the lips.
Glorious birdsong upon the heart.
Tomorrows that transcend time.
Yet halos circumvent the demon's horns.

Angelic heart dreaming in the stars.
With crimson paint upon the walls
Broken hearts and fresh earth,
As the sun stops time.

Oh, trio of words
Why did you tease my soul.
And fuel the burning flames.
I LOVE YOU?

Illustrator James Penn

Chains

Cumbersome and heavy,
Lying in unorganized piles.
Scattered around the fool's bedside.
Keeping out those who dare to enter.

Dreary chains of love.
Mincing the amorous nights,
And foolishly obliterating sweet good nights.
Replaced by darkness and shadow's delight.

Demon's mockery, fed by soot-covered pots.
Shadow's mist, teasing the flames.
As the night sheds its cloak.
And the cool breeze singes the tear-soaked filters.

Gasping, groping for an ounce of something,
Pulling at the chains, hugging them tightly.
Praying for morn's light,
While embracing the love of cold, cold steel

Illustrator James Penn

Tombstone Mentality

As the waning sun rises,
The darkness creeps in.
Gathering the wings from the soul,
Smothering the love with foul dirt.

The stench of the morning's dew,
Reminds the heart of imminent hell.
If only the grave would be so kind,
As to smother the dying flame.

Dreams begging for the reality,
The reality of a name left for all time.
Written in stone for all to see.
Left for the birds to perch upon.

Dreams of sleep so sweet.
A dream without the agony of love.
Fairytales dying at the shovel's tip.
As the last teardrop falls.

Falter not, oh, dark shadow,
For your friendship I have accepted.
Let your robe protect my soul,
From the tyranny of love.

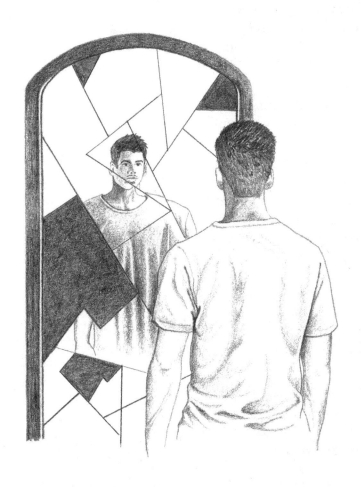

Illustrator James Penn

Blackened Mirror

Dreams of love reflecting life.
Imaginary lies of a blackened mirror,
Promising fairy tales and forever
For the stricken fool's heart.

Anger and disappointment,
Casting the looking glass.
Upon the floor perfect dreams
Scatter to the wind, thousands of shards.

Painful, broken memories
Piercing an angel's feet.
Fallacies and wishes draining the life,
A broken dream at a time.

"If only" and "what if" mock the night.
Her happiness, not from love's spell.
As the tears drown the blood.
And the blood reminds the heart.

The enchanted heart dreams of its mate.
As its mate longs for another's lies.
Walking to and fro upon the bed of glass,
Self-made lies adorn the morning's glimmer.

As the remaining love and final prayer leave.
The weakened soul dies one last time.
A final farewell, as time forbids
And the lights fade one final time.

Merdemon

Ice-cold river,
Burning a path through her veins
Branding a mark on the soul.
Eternity stolen by her eyes.

Heartless demon scouring the seas
Gnawing at the sailors' flesh.
Silent screams begging,
Pleading for an ounce of love.

Only crumbs from the table,
Fell from where the family ate.
Little hope could be felt
As bones crumbled to dust.

Silently screaming, mercies' cry,
As the day drags to night.
Not a peep, not a crack or crevice.
As her armor shines through the night.

Mended Heart

My heart breaks for the tears
The tears you shed through the years

My soul despises the pain
That left such an inglorious stain

The demons may have become an integral part
But now is the time to remove them from your heart

A special heart can share
If your soul you dare to bare

But be not afraid, my friend
For this is nowhere near the end

Joy is only around the bend
For the stars have made sure you will mend

Death

How many more hours shall I search?

For thee

How many more pleas shall I send?

Upon my knees

Why is your stain not upon my door?

As my screams beg

Where are you tonight?

Oh,

Death bless me with thy mercy.

And quench the candle's light

Can You Love Me

Oh, but the pain
Loving the unwilling heart.

Loneliness captures the night
As the mirror reflects not.

Endless days
Captivated with darkness

Peering into the empty eyes
Of a love-darkened soul.

Love

Dry broken lips
Squelching for the words
To fill the mind's soul
With peace and love

Glorious sunrises
Imparting life
Gracing a tortured soul
With mercy and hope

Jumping boldly
Playfully splashing
No fear, no shame, no guilt
Only childish dreams

Dreams, searching
For one moment of hope
Passion filling the lungs
With the first breath of life

LOVE

FOREVER

AND EVER

Silence

Silence
As an angel falls

From heaven,
Into broken arms
Captured,
With love and immortal embrace

Gentle spirits
Guided by darkness
Now endowed by love's light
Paved roads of the widow's sight

Rocking back and forth
As the days sway by
Memories searching for forgiveness
As the dust crumbles beneath

Gentle old hands
Weathered and torn
Anxious for the morning light
As love gathers another day.

Dry Pockets

Fuck the tears that burnt a hole in my soul.
Fuck the years that took away my youth.

To hell with tomorrow and the days to come
Leaving it all on the sheets tonight.

Screw the pain and the agony you dumped on me.
Going to obliterate the nightmares at Satan's feet.

Keep your rivers in your dry pockets.
Moisten not the skies with your writings,
For it never mattered more than...

Oceans of Green

From the heavens a star fell.
Fell upon my lap.
Glorious gift from God
Perfection in my arms

Pristine oceans of green
Mesmerizing the night's air.
Captivating the heart
The heart of the ravaged soul.

Sweet melody of the wind
Pirouetting down the Angel's wings.
Such a beautiful melodic voice
Ringing melodies into the night.

Kisses blessed by the stars
As rain sweetens the passion
Lost, lost in a moment
Eternal bliss parading at the fingertips

Dancing in the Rain

Have you ever danced in the rain?
Gazing a thousand miles into the soul of the one in your arms.
Forgetting the day, and living in the moment as your bodies become
    one.
Surrounded by no more than an eternal memory.
No music, no sounds, except the beating of our hearts.
Each drop of rain washing away the world around us.
Each drop giving birth to a new page and a new chapter of love and
    ecstasy.
Silly moments of passion flooding a new love with glorious
heartfelt desires.

Chains

Chains around my wings
Chains lining the soul of my heart
Clouds taking the shape
The shape of chains

The future tied,
Tied by the chains
The past drug along
Drug by the chains

Wretched ungodly beasts
Wrapped around my neck
Choking the wind
And robbing the smile

When shall you let me breathe
Breathe the life
The life back into my lungs
Returning life after death

Make It Rain on Me

Make it rain,
Make it rain your love
Till I'm feeling no pain.
A little slice of heaven from above

Make it rain,
Make it rain happiness
Till in your arms I belong
Angel's wings spreading your love

Make it rain,
Make it rain your sexy smile
Till at home I feel
Make it rain, make it rain you

Loneliness

Ungreased wheels on my chair,
No one to push, no one to pull,
Rolling, struggling to get out of the room
A room with no light and no direction.

A room with no floors,
Only heavy rains seeping into the ground
Fighting to pull the wheels, another round,
Stuck in the clingy clay swamps

No sounds, but the beating of the heart.
Deafening, piercing the drums with screams.
Thousands upon thousands of voices
Taunting and teasing, but no one in sight

Oddity of friends gather 'round.
Droplets of blood running down the arm
Each gaining its own name.
Razors become an invite to friendship

A bug in the corner, a man that doesn't exist.
Friends long since gone
And notes left to yourself.
Become a ray of hope, but nothing more.

Morning's light mocks the soul
A reminder that no one is here.
Courage and cowardice go hand in hand
As the blade sends the RSVP

Tempestuous Smile

Bloodstained cards
And
Crispy brown rose petals
Line the floor of the morbid crypt

Picture-perfect memories
Tile the path
With the evening's hell
Wound around forgotten promises.

Crimson-soaked tools
Marks left in the Angel's wings.
Death
And imprisonment await.

Prayers and pleas
Resentment for the morning's light.
Rivers of torment
Dreamers swim for shore

Curse the day
And
Torch the night owl
Hell soothes the soul with fire.

Happiness found
At the razor's edge
Perched upon death's sword
Mortal rivers drown the smile

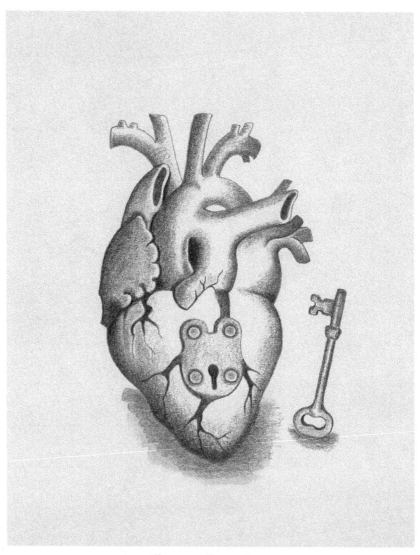

Illustrator James Penn

The Key

Over and over, I searched the house.
Looking in all the drawers.
Searching under the couch
Removing the cushions.

I went through the laundry
And took it all out of the closet.
I looked under all the mats,
And searched all the high shelves.

I searched each room in desperation.
Shed tear after tear knowing all was lost.
I called friends and family
Even looked in the dog's bed.

I had all but given up when I knew
I knew I had one last chance.
So if you would
And if you could

Please tell me where you put the key.
The chain is smothering each breath.
The lock has become so heavy.
And no one has been able to remove it.

I want so bad to give my heart to others.
But you hid the key.
Why would you do that to me?
Why can't you let me be free?

Acidic Tears

Upon my cheeks
For the world to see.
Debossed deeply
Agony and weariness
Linger in the dry rivers.

Endless nights
No sleep in sight
Heart knocking on death's door
Morning's light
Evil's terrifying fright.

Burning a path
In love's aftermath
Torture defined by wrath
Spelling out a demon's path
Washed in the bloody bath.

Pillows soaked in tears
Releasing nightly fears
Sheets divided by daggers and spears
Stacked upon Satan's piers
As the glorious end nears.

Happiness avails
As the night's air becomes stale
Love once again will fail
Open the daily mail
And receive the morning's hell

Crazy Bird

As the sun arose today
I sat upon the grass
The grass so green.

The breeze blew so gentle
I looked up in the sky
The sky so blue

There was an odd bird
Backward he flew
Flew from whence he came.

For a moment I watched
I watched in dismay
As backward he flew.

From the old bird
An answer I pleaded
Tell me, tell me please

Why is it backward you fly?
How will you ever get where you going?
If backward you fly.

Rain showers falling from the sky.
Created from the tears he cried.
Out of breath, he bravely answered.

"Down there upon the ground
Trees and rocks bruise your path
And refuse your sight for tomorrow.

But it is up here so high
So high above the world so cold
That I can see all that is about to be."

Again I asked the old bird
So why is it backward you fly?
What has you so afraid of tomorrow?

He squawked, "I have seen from where you came.
And I have seen where you are.
Yet it is what is ahead that frightens me.

The sun that comes,
Comes from the darkest corners.
Now is covered, covered in blood."

As backward from sight he flew.
His wings pleaded with the wind.
"Take me back, back to the happiness I knew."

As I sat upon the grass.
The grass so green.
All was...

Old Friend

Apologies, my friend

It has been a while,
I'm sure you thought,
I had found a different style.

You are back in my arms again
I know you thought I was gone.
But time made sure love was slain.

Memories of her
Plaguing my mind
Have made my speech slur.

Forgive me and find your way,
Search deep and make your home
This time, your edge is here to stay.

It will be our little secret path
This time no one will know
Of the internal wrath.

Make your mark for those to see
Let them know what is in me
Your pain will bring me such glee.

Forgive my time away
Never will I let you down
Because I no longer want to stay

Illustrator Bryon Redfield

Do We Cry Together

Why must I sit here in this bed?
Believing that we cry together.
Miles and miles between us yet,
I believe that the rivers that I shed
will meet the rivers that you shed.

Why must I believe that you care?
Why should I even dream?
Dream a dream that you dream,
A dream of me.

Yet night after night
I sleep upon the bloody pool
Amassed by the razor's edge.
As my friends taunt me and tease me.

Do you dream the dreams I dream?
As you lie in his arms.
Is it the love I showed you?
That brings you back to my arms each night.

I know you dream no more
Your heart no longer feels the feelings
The feelings of love I had for you.
As my soul loved your soul.

My only love now
Is the love of pain
Pain has become my life
And mortal wound shall set me free

Passion

Darkened room
Dimly lit candle
Flickering to the beat
The beat of the night's love

Gentle soft breath
Pulled passionately
Softly
Across the neck

Tingling touch
Upon the hips
Shivers down the spine
Uncontrollable twitches

Joined,
Deeply,
Sweating and moaning
Breathing as one.

Painful pleasure
Locks pulled so tight.
Gentle ecstasy
Mmm

Reaching for…
Again she's gone
Empty arms
Love is dead.

Value

Is it the fool's penny?
Or is it the debutante's dollar?

Could it be the tears shed?
Shed from a heart of love

Maybe the fancy gems
Or the shiny toys?

Surely it was the tiny acts
The acts of love and compassion.

Was it the fool on the steed?
Believing he could ever be enough.

If none of these?
Then nothing could ever please.

Describe the value of a fool in love.
Was it not enough to promise death for life?

Claw the eyes from the beast.
Rake the loins clean of flesh.

Crawl through the mire and muck
Meander the path through hell's journey.

The value has been decided by those that received
Decided when they said goodbye.

Illustrator Bryon Redfield

Written in Stone

On a hot summer's day,
Happiness refused to play.
I sat alone in the dark.
Remnants of love left its mark.

As from the shadows I gazed,
The lonely heart was left amazed.
Tear-soaked knees struggled with the name.
Why did he have to leave the game?

I screamed and I cried,
Once again it felt like I died.
Please hold me! Don't leave me here!
As my reddened eyes shed a tear.

Written in stone, memories of yesteryear.
Unanswered questions forgotten in tears.
Trodden paths wallowed in the grass.
Memories forgotten as times pass.

How many days should the soul torment?
As the agony continues to ferment.
As one after the other they come by.
Screams are silenced with a gentle sigh.

As before, I reached out my arms.
But no one saw any harm.
Each name I screamed intently
From my company they parted innocently

Breath still filled my rotten lung
Even though the final bell had been rung.
Please do not leave, for the air becomes so sour
shortly after the visiting hour.

Hidden Treasure

Screams of steel,
Parting the night air
Like a ghost ship
And the morning's fog.

Dead man's gold,
Buried below,
Hidden, awaiting
The razor's bounty

Bloodshed,
Arms holding the hope
One more passionate cut
And the treasure's home.

Dig, for the course,
Shall show the light,
The lighted path
As the blood flows

Love is forgotten,
As the blade makes its home
Deeper and deeper,
The cuts become.

When shall the pain die?
Is it when the pain becomes
Becomes too strong?
Or when the flow stops?

Intertwined

Alone I shall be,
But alone will not grant me peace.
In the dark many shall come,
Comfort, the least of their desires.

Memories they will flood,
Pain and anguish, limits of sanity
Hand in hand desperate journeys.
Little room for else do they leave.

Unreasonable ventures to the depths.
Journeys to the mind's soul.
Forgotten friend lost in the storm.
What path his heart has taken?

Happiness and sadness
Closest of friends for eternity
Each day shall be the last
But no end shall ever bless.

Evil spell casting lots
Spoken words and deep thoughts
Price paid in blood
Happiness finally bought.

I Had Rather Went Blind

I had rather went blind.

Than to see you leave.

No one seems to understand.

No one seems to know the feeling.

So many times I felt your wrath. So many times you hugged me
tightly as I cried myself to sleep. The ropes choked the wind
from my lungs. The nails pierced holes in my heart. Never a
drop on the sheets, but I cried rivers of red as the life left my
soul. Soon I lost sight of who I was. My existence became no
more the pain that you induced.

You smiled so deeply,

You promised tomorrow and tomorrow's tomorrows.

You made me feel so loved and desired.

The love lied without a blink. And the pain became my life. I awoke
with the needle in my arm, and I went to bed with the straw in
my nose. Each dose created a desire, desire for more of your pain,
and worse pain. The stories of all the men, that had molested
my fantasy, raped my dreams. The stories made it all so dirty.
Shower after shower failed to wash the blood from our love.

I came on my knees.

I crawled and begged like an addict.

I hated the breath you breathed.

When there was no mercy left. Like a thief in the night. You stole the only thing that kept me alive. Now it is in other eyes that I'm liked. I see perfection, but it scares me to death. I need the pain. I need the misery. I need the torture. I became dependent. I became an addict. Now I live restrained to a couch, bound by what little pain my memories grasp to hold.

They tell me to stop.

They tell me to find happiness.

They tell me life will be okay.

It is the trampling of my heart that kept me alive. How am I supposed to live without it? The nights I hate, the demons run rampant. But it is the only place I feel safe. No one left in my life, but those that eat my very soul.

Why can't someone love me?

Why can't anyone see how great I am?

Why can't they finish the job before morrow's light?

Blue Seas

Passionate deep blue seas
Weigh the anchor
Hoist the sails
Set your bearings
Forever island awaits

Be not afraid
The night hides no demons
All can be beat
Head into the wind
Break the waves

Get lost in the dark
Deep, deep blue sea
Passion at her fingertips
Embrace the embraces
Overcome the waves

Stay the course
Chart the island
And find the gold
For her heart
Will ever be yours

And the World Turns to Blood

Rivers fading into the sun.
Defying logic as they turn red.
Picturesque mountains lose their glory
As anger turns the snow rosy.

And the world turns to blood.

Visions of what used to be,
And what could have been.
Replaced with the orange glow of the fire,
As the devil rakes the coals of sleep.

And the world turns to blood.

Side by side captured forever in time,
As the pages turn forward and back.
Memories no longer bring the smiles,
Just fear as the avalanches crush life.

And the world turns to blood.

The daggers of your words
Rip and burn their way into the night
Never to feel the warmth of your arms.
You say you don't feel that way.

And the world turns to blood.

Can I ever remove the ink,
From my brain and cleanse it all?
As time moves forward,
And my heart stands still.

And the world turns to blood

Why

A fading memory
A longing for a breath of air
Time grows weary
As the hands spin 'round and 'round

Visions of a smile
Reflecting back at me
Glorious rays of eternal flowers
All about the world

Searching for my heart
Darkest of nights
Not a prayer in sight
Why?

Why?

Why?

Why must the heart love so deep?
Why can no one see the gifts to bear?
Why must the mountain be so steep?
Why must the world, oh, gentle heart tear?

Dreams upon dreams, upon dreams
So much love willing to share.
Ripping at the seams,
To the world it does bare.

One kind heart, faith has been lost
No glory to a bended knee.
Weakness and shameless love
Quicker the end will be found.

Why?

Late-Night Dances

Empty walls
And
Empty halls

Empty bed
And
Empty arms

No one to wipe the tears
And
No one to share the smiles

No more good-morning kisses
And
No more morning breath

No more late-night crazies
And
No more breathless moments

No more hello's
And
No more goodbyes

No more chances
And
No more late-night dances.

Only
The devil
And
His evil prances.

True Love (10x)

Tempestuous journeys
To a land that
Fails to exist
Eternally

Pure of Heart

Drip…

Drip…

To the floor love falls
Tomorrow's yesterdays
Standing
Still in time.

Passion embodied,
Captured by finality.
Tortured by time,
And Seduced by death.

Blackened wings
Vengeance upon the innocent
Promises and
Promises

Love conquers all
By the sword's edge.
Strong mind's game
Devouring

The
Pure
At
Heart

First Love

Is it humanity that breeds life into love?
Or Is it love that breeds humanity unto life?
What is it about love that requires humanity?
Is it not possible to feel love as if a God?

Oh, the simple nectar that cultivates life,
While a wooden stake pierces the heart with words.
Dangling forever upon mysteries of the deep blue,
As passion lights the path's torch.

The fear of the first move toward eternity,
As a father's call lingers in the forgotten corners.
Gentle glimpses showered with moonlit dust.
As Angel's wings quench the jitters with lust.

Exquisite walks as the sand tickles the toes.
Hand in hand, hearts saunter toward morn.
An array of words lost in night,
As eyes and heartbeats fill the glass.

A pitiful soliloquy portrayed with lumbering words.
Visions of tomorrow masked by a moment's heat.
Sweetest lips embodying the emotions of the heart
As heaven facilitates the sweetest of words

I LOVE YOU!

The Carriage Arrives

As the ricochet of your pain has castrated the wind from my lungs, my lips parched and blue beg and gasp. Darkness encroaches and the beasts perch upon my chest. Rivers toppling the rocks in desperate pleas for life. Demons devouring daylight's solitude with angry howls and invisible fangs. The devil's nefarious orchestra warming for a perilous journey. Daylight brings no peace, for fear lingers on. Oh, but for a moment's blink, a tiny draw through the cracks in the claws. Even if only to wet the lips with taste of air. Greed asks not for a breath, just cries and cries for the remembrance of fresh air. Oh, but your love has so tainted the Divine equity that filled the lungs with dreams. Now each breath tattoos agony and engrained hatred upon the soul. It is not your soul that is hated. Hatred comes for your lack of sympathy. Why did you not drive the dagger deeper into its sheath? Planned out your torture was, but sweet death you would not give. The voices they cannot hear, but understood they well are. Methodic chants of death's door and the hinges of pain harmonize as they sing a siren's song. Eleven more days till the fiery carriage arrives. Seductive horses tamping an irresistible call. Into the darkness dust they scatter. Silence and happiness are their gifts.

My Arms around You

The feeling of being alone still haunts
My mind
First time I saw you still excites
My heart

I can still see your beauty with
My eyes
Your skin I can still feel with
My hand

The moment you said yes
Time stood still
As my arms wrapped around you
I felt safe

For the first time, I could feel
Real love
For the first time, my body didn't
Feel abused

The only time I couldn't feel my abusers
Touching me
All I could feel was myself
Inside you

Finally, I felt my heart beat
With yours
Finally, my mind was free
From pain

Never would I have believed
Et tu brute
Now another looks in
Your eyes

As upon the pillow my
Blood spills
And in the final
Night

My body screams for the shelter
Of your arms
My ears scream for
Your voice

But you aren't there
Are you?
You left me alone and
To die

Your wish shall finally
Come true
Your desires have
Shown through

I meant nothing
To you
I was only shelter and money in
Your pocket

Now watch as my friends
Line up
To only see my face in
Their dreams

Now you can watch as
They carry me away
Alive or dead
I am worthless

For you took
My heart
And my soul died
That day

Friendship

I'll throw you a line if
gentle with my heart you shall be
accepting of my spirit wild and free
as understanding, pain took

We all need friends, so I'll throw a lifeline
forever my heart you shall have the key
I want to know the line's strong so give me a sign
with love make your days mine
and hold tight to the friendship line
forever in eternity intertwined

Illustrator Kirsten Fay

A Good Woman

Please!
Tell me where the good is
Give all that a man can offer
And upon your heart they trample

Share the depths of your soul
And nothing will stop them
From pain they came
To hell they will send you

Why would the heart
Torture itself with foolish attempts
By now it should know
That love doesn't exist.

How much more should I leave?
How many more deaths shall I suffer?
Before my heart shall see
Alone I will die

Why Did God not create one
Not one good woman did he...
Love was the heart's desire
But offers little more than death

If one good woman fortune holds
Embrace her tight and never let her go
A fool you shouldn't be
For there will never be another.

So Sweet Is Your Name

So sweet is your name
Gently crossing my tongue
With visions of love

So beautiful are your eyes
The stories they tell
With visions of love

So perfect is your voice
Tempting my heart to fall
With visions of love

So gentle is your touch
Sending tingles down my spine
With visions of love

So amazing are the thoughts
Of you and I dancing alone
With visions of love

Oh, but the sweetest of moments
Looking deep into your eyes
With visions of love

And love and love
And love

Illustrator Kirsten Fay

Paper Cage

Oh, words fail me not
For there has to be a greater plot
Let my tongue guide the way
So the memory will ever stay

Passionate words twisted in rhyme
Makin' sweet love last for all time
Visions and thoughts pouring from the pen
Captured eternity for all men

Misunderstood words upon the page
Captured forever in the paper cage
Stories of how sweet the love
Glory manifest from far above

Never more will this be sought
For hereafter it will only be taught
Poetry and dreams exposed for the sad
Loneliness and love never goes bad

Happy people live for the song
It seems to make them strong
For the notes they plea
In heaven they shall be

For the sinister twister of words
Nothing greater than the darkest birds
Line after line words unite
Such a glorious painful sight

Not for glory or fame
Do we reveal darkest shame
Casting a spell for eternity
A brotherhood and forever fraternity

Illustrator Bryon Redfield

What Should I Write

What should I write with words tonight?
Should I write that demons dance in flight?
Maybe the stars are no longer in the sky
But that would only tell a lie

Don't be silly the stars never left the heavens
Although I'm sure I saw a dragon with heads of seven
Those around can't see the end has come
Yet Satan has put my heart under her thumb.

Remember the days that my life was love
Now the winds have made me void of
So passionate was her smile
Now, nothing could be more vile

Through such a tiny void he came
Before long, I was the one to blame
Upon the sultry eyes I never laid
All the cards had done been played

Search hard for the fiery grave
Each day is such a close shave
A gentle knock on the doors of death
Screaming impatiently for the final breath

They all doubt that death will show its head
I can assure that I will soon be dead
Tomorrow's light is not my friend
Nothing more glorious than the end

Oh, the miles she rode upon her back
As my nights went to a deeper black
A few short days from now
And the last rows I shall plow

From the earth will come no seed
The heavens did make the heart bleed
At the days end, there will be no harvest
Words spoke louder and louder that I do not jest

As the page turns
And the hearts burn
Layer the clouds ever so thick
Never more have I been so sick

Make the bed upon the hill
And lay the love upon the seal
To the fool it may seem to bend
Yet only one prayer needs to send

The arms will pull close tonight
Finally an end to the horrific fright
Give it all the final seed
For in pain her heart will bleed.

She Returns

As the day slips unto forgotten, the darkness overtakes the peace. Serenity slowly becomes agony, and love fades with the light. The angels among us return to their homes, and the ravens sharpen their claws. Tightly wrapped sheets tangle and confuse the soul. Reluctantly, the eyes grow weary, and the battlefield emerges. Each night, she returns to tease and taunt. Reminding the heart that the arms hug a vapor. Prancing to and fro, pacing across the heart with thunderous steps, she reminds of us the absence of presence. Without care or remorse, the demons pull and pluck the fading memories, leaving an empty soul. That's my wife! Silent screams beg the night and yearn for morning's light.

Cry Not for Me

Unto the heavens reached the shaking hand. Bound by earthly teth-
ers, yearned for a broken heart. Passionate words, fathers' desires,
and screams woke the morning's light. Blinded ears and deafened
eyes searched for heaven's sight. Hidden words softened the soil, yet
the feet failed to break free. Consuming swamps swallowed the final
drop of pride as bended knees met the lonely earth. A downward
glance brought forth the emptiness that swallowed the final breath.
Upon the neck, breath fell not as eyes failed to cross. Shame brought
forth endless lies and visions of pearls upon the face of the wicked
angels. Truth upon the ears could not be seen as the pain engulfed the
heart. Cry not for me! Cry not for me! Ravenous tears burned their
mark, almost winning the weary heart. Fail me not, oh, gentle path,
for nothing lies in the aftermath.

About the Author

Photographer Amber Bolejack

The author grew up in the hills of Southern Appalachia and traveled much of the South in the military. Living in states such as Mississippi, North Carolina, Virginia, and Texas, he gained cultural experiences and a had few loves in his life. As most of us know, with love comes pain. This pain has been converted into carefully chosen words to explain his feelings. He often leaves his work raw and untouched to keep it as real as possible. The author in his early years was described as a struggling student. Lack of focus and direction was often used to describe him. A few minor school assignments showed hidden feelings and emotions leeching their way to the outside. Thirty years later and endless bottled-up emotions exploded and the words in this book were delicately laced onto every napkin and wrinkled piece of paper within the weathered grasp. Carefully hidden yet cautiously preserved, these poems stayed a painful secret and reminder of the tormented past. It was only after much thought and encouragement that a decision was made to release the collection that is before you. The author hopes that the collection and all future books shared will illustrate that you are not alone and that your feelings are shared by many more.

Printed in the USA
CPSIA information can be obtained
at www.ICGtesting.com
LVHW091154081124
795950LV00003B/414

* 9 7 9 8 8 9 3 0 8 3 0 0 2 *